TRIALS
&
TRIBULATIONS

Rayne Lopez-Gamboa

Rayne Lopez-Gamboa

For *you*

Rayne Lopez-Gamboa

CONTENTS

presentation of evidence..4

witness testimony..30

cross examination...61

closing argument...83

Rayne Lopez-Gamboa

CASE #91897

YOU VS.
YOUR STATE OF MIND

Presentation of Evidence

"i have a hunch that i might be two different people"

destined to stay stagnant
my ghosts lurk in the corners
and undo any good that was coming my way
i sit in agony and wish for fate to write me a different
ending
only thanking karma for giving me what I deserve
it seems insignificant in the moment but comes back to
haunt me
my tendencies to be impulsive
the tiny notches that make up the timeline
come together finally at the pinnacle
and i realize that no one but me has played a hand in
my demise
i've been hopeful since i was a child
that things might go my way
and it's that silly thought
that keeps bringing me to my knees
again and again

Rayne Lopez-Gamboa

suddenly a wave of it hits me
the current of it is so strong
my heart acts as an anchor
pulling me down where it thinks i belong
and i've always struggled with floating
while others do it with ease
i wonder if it's just me that can't grasp it
or if i was born with a missing piece

slowly i look behind me
my heart racing from anxiety
suspicion clouding my judgment
my breath is still for silence
i heard a sound in the distance
another pair of footsteps
someone following me slowly
who somehow knows where i'm going
caught a glimpse in my peripheral
it was a hooded figure with a sickle

Rayne Lopez-Gamboa

i'm guilty of existing
taking up space
being a wallflower
trying to blend in
but things keep changing
and i'm constantly thrown forward
forced to face problems head on
leaving me exhausted
because i never planned
to live past my 18th birthday

Rayne Lopez-Gamboa

i'm not very good at choosing who to trust
so i'd rather not trust at all

Rayne Lopez-Gamboa

i'm sorry i'm not the optimist
but smiling feels like being stabbed
i'm sorry i don't take part in laughter
because it tastes like eating ash
and as i wait for the subway
i'll look back just once more
at the girls on the bench gossiping
knowing that was me before

Rayne Lopez-Gamboa

my demon still keeps me hostage
it doesn't help that i know its name

Rayne Lopez-Gamboa

in the darkness
staring at the ceiling
i remind myself
this is the life i chose
this is the life i chose

i still think about places and people
that have long forgotten about me

my demon thrives on suspicion
it makes me question your every move

i must be dreaming
dreaming that i was meant for something bigger
that the lines on the palms of my hands
meant i'd be great
and the stars placement
when i was born
promised me success
my biggest fear is that
they did not promise me
anything

i wish to reflect on nothing
but the memories flood me anyway

how many times did i wish
to leave it all behind
yet still chained by the red string
that connected their souls to my life

Rayne Lopez-Gamboa

let me fade
if it's time
so that i can absorb
and rot
in synchronicity

once i arrived i was bathed
in the golden light
the speckled shadows from the tree branches
dotted my face and hands
i reached out to touch the grass
lush and infinite
each blade its own color and length
would plucking one disturb the others
even so momentarily
quickly compensating for their loss
or would this patch of grass never be the same
without it

Rayne Lopez-Gamboa

all i can think about
is how good a bullet would taste in my mouth
like lemonade on a hot summer day
or a warm bowl of soup in the fall
i bet it would taste like mashed potatoes
maybe a steak or thanksgiving meal
i'd be full and satisfied
looking down at my empty plate
pain
pleasure
it's all the same

i've had this feeling now for years
that the demons clouding my vision
are here to stay for good
the shadows that creep in the daytime
will never cross to the other side
i'll never know where they came from
although i probably have an idea
this sickness is in my bloodstream
it's a manifestation of the past
i've dreamed one day it won't matter
i've tried to stifle it as best i can
but the beckoning of the climax
hangs overhead even so
i'll have to embrace this sense of madness
it's better than waiting for the unknown
the clock ticks silently
but the bomb will still explode

Rayne Lopez-Gamboa

i naively assumed
no one would outgrow me
that im compatible to those i love
but i know a fact to be true and inevitable
intersecting lines will always become parallel

is there nothing i won't let you do to me?
i shouted
i grabbed my face in my hands
and whispered
there isn't

Rayne Lopez-Gamboa

one of my biggest faults is
thinking that talking to myself
counts as having a friend

Rayne Lopez-Gamboa

im forced to watch
and my hands are tied
as someone who looks like me
wreaks havoc on my life

Rayne Lopez-Gamboa

there is an incessant ringing in my ears
that is why i never trust face value

Rayne Lopez-Gamboa

i woke up atop a mountain
my soul took me to the summit
and it begged me to correct my ways
instead i ignored it
standing at the edge
overwhelmed with the beauty
could i be like that? i asked with tears in my eyes
one day it replied
if you changed

Rayne Lopez-Gamboa

it's pointless to wish for things that won't happen
i torture myself with the outcomes
silently observing the past
in a blink i've lived every possibility
the present becomes my nemesis
passive, a dormant promise that remains unclaimed
each day is wasted by living in it
wading in tainted water chest deep
i know that hindsight is a deadly assassin
it relishes to execute me repeatedly
i'm aware there aren't many ways to fight it
rather i must lay down and die
and although bleeding out is imminent
i'll be revived instantaneously once more
among others unaware of the internal struggle
to continue the life i selected
out of the thousands i could have chosen

Rayne Lopez-Gamboa

an overabundance was harvested
i have so much rotten fruit
i boast of their excellence
while actively concealing the truth
now everyone wants a bite
of my expired fruit

Rayne Lopez-Gamboa

Witness

Testimony

"ive seen parts of myself that should have remained hidden"

Rayne Lopez-Gamboa

i've seen the ocean twice
the first time was the pacific when i was 9
the second time was in your eyes when i met you

Rayne Lopez-Gamboa

if winter comes and you still haven't called
i'll go outside no shoes or coat
reminding myself that being out in the snow
was as the same as being with you
frigid and alone

Rayne Lopez-Gamboa

having you next to me
didn't fill the void
i thought it would
instead it dug a deeper hole
i fell into

in the grand scheme of things
i suppose it's better to have known your love
for the blip of this existence
than leave my soul yearning
in this life
and every life after

Rayne Lopez-Gamboa

i often wonder if it will be all for nothing
our moments shared stored away in bookshelves
a mental scrapbook
our holy spaces covered in cobwebs
a hole in my chest, unsewn, gaping open
like the mouth of an enemy slain
it's a slow burn to the skin
so i stay alert when there is no danger
but still i must remember
the beauty of impermanence is this
offering and earning are infinite

Rayne Lopez-Gamboa

but how can i not think of you
when i'm living inside of a body
you've touched

and been inside of

and breathed into

Rayne Lopez-Gamboa

oh my god i'm so scared
that one day i'll see you look at her
like you planted a garden in her lungs
after burying me alive
and i'll be suffocating

while she's breathing flowers into your neck

and your eyes
they weren't empty
just more like half full

Rayne Lopez-Gamboa

every time
i close my eyes
it's like
i'm there
again
and i'm still
unsure
if it's heaven
or hell
i keep reliving

Rayne Lopez-Gamboa

and the truth is
i'll still pray to you
even after
you've shown me
you're satan

begging for something that won't happen
i'm too romantic and unrealistic
plagued by high expectations
grasping at unfinished sentences
like loose cliff stone it gives way
i'm expected to take the fall with grace
but there is no safe place to land

Rayne Lopez-Gamboa

the lips i never kissed consumed me

slowly it died
giving out a whimper
after all the years of feeding it
i watched its rib cage
heave one final time
and the light leave its eyes
the piece of me where i kept it
aching just a twinge
a tear escaped
just for a moment
it was finally dead
i win

Rayne Lopez-Gamboa

i always wished of sleeping next to you
the warmth of your body lulling me into dreams
and now finally realized
my anxious heart is at ease

Rayne Lopez-Gamboa

your mouth was the sweetest sin i could have tasted
a delicacy i can't afford again

Rayne Lopez-Gamboa

i don't wish to be adored
i simply wish to be understood

i read our conversations at night like scripture
because you're one damn holy being
and in the morning i'm spent and jaded
remembering what you've said to me
so when you ask how i've slept tomorrow
i am going to tell you fine
but if you asked me what we talked about
i could recite it back one hundred times

Rayne Lopez-Gamboa

the brush of your lips against mine
felt like flowers in full bloom
and the sky on that night above us
i won't ever forget
was a full moon
and maybe the chill in the air was warning me
instead of trying to coax me into your arms
i should have stopped your advances but fuck
your breath on my neck was so warm

i saw your words as they formed in the cold air
a ghostly fog in the middle of the night
i hope you know i think of that all the time

Rayne Lopez-Gamboa

There's something about your soul
I've known it before

Rayne Lopez-Gamboa

if miles were measured in heartbeats
at least i'd be able to feel the distance
because looking at a map feels empty
as i trace my fingertips along the highways
that seem to be my veins
reaching toward your town

Rayne Lopez-Gamboa

i see your silhouette in the living room
it's almost like i can touch you
the sun peeking out past the curtains
a ghost in daytime view
a pattern of lines and shapes
that make up all of you
i retreat with you to the mattress
no problem, especially for us
and nothing else exists because
have i died yet?
it can't be, but you're so close to me
have i died yet?
you must be heaven sent
in this bedroom
god has spoken through your fingertips

i guess im just so scared of the universe
that i convinced myself
we could make our own
when im aware that there's a world full of passion
and hunger pulling at your bones

Rayne Lopez-Gamboa

my nails on your back
i hope they've left a scar
when she asks
you'll have to tell her what they are

i will know i am healed when
i can look you in the eyes
and say *it's good to see you again*

i've writhed long enough internally
there are days when i detonate
i met someone who taught me
rage is necessary and human

Rayne Lopez-Gamboa

just looking at a picture of you
i can easily taste your neck
and i wish nothing more than
for me to forget

Rayne Lopez-Gamboa

when you've finished
you move to the other side of the bed
my skin cries
more
more
more

our love was simply whispered
covered by the sounds in the distance
a show of fireworks overhead
i rested my chin on your shoulder
and i still miss the feel of your hand
holding me down into the mattress
the finale comes to fruition

maybe i held you too tightly or not enough i can't
figure out which
nothing i think seems to metastasize into coherent
sentences anymore
just images and fragments of thought that don't last for
more than a millisecond
im so fucking tired
i can't keep my eyes open but i can't stay asleep either
It's impossible to tell if it's because missing you wakes
me up
or my brain is intentionally sabotaging itself
my mouth tastes like iron; blood
it cakes my lips in the morning
it sticks to my skin like a leech clinging to a host
theres a bigger part of me that yearns for this to cease
but the rest of me believes that if there's no pain then
none of this was real
there will be no reminder those moments ever existed
hot breath evaporating into nothing on a cold day
that would be the end of us truly
the forgetting

Rayne Lopez-Gamboa

Cross Examination

"defending myself was always harder than it had to be"

Rayne Lopez-Gamboa

while the road looks the same
the journey will hopefully differ
i'm tired of walking down the same path
wishing for a different destination
when i always end up in the same kinds of places
with the same kinds of people
and wonder how i got here
when my legs are the ones that have carried me
slowly staggering up the steps of that decrepit chapel
i open the gates expecting to be welcomed with open arms
but instead i'm greeted by spirits that refuse to cross over
and challenges i thought i'd already won

Rayne Lopez-Gamboa

i see their quick glances at each other
as i stumble over my words
more proof im inadequate
and a bullet is the only cure

Rayne Lopez-Gamboa

i say i lost 30 pounds
people ask me how i did it
how do I tell them that i was up all night worrying
about bills instead of worried about what to make for
breakfast
how do i tell them that i live off the bag of bottle
deposits in my kitchen
how do i tell them i keep losing because i can't afford to
be full
learning to ignore the hunger
just two more days
just one more day
still empty

i tell them i quit eating carbs

i try to wriggle free from the clutches
of who im supposed to be
expected to take each blow in stride
like the ones before me
but im not that person
and i wont ever be
when i get cut
im not vengeful
i just bleed

Rayne Lopez-Gamboa

here i go again charging full speed without looking both ways
i always choose flight over fight when it comes to situations I didn't prepare for
if all the masks i have curated over time don't fit the scene
instead of becoming someone new on the spot
my old self wriggles its way to surface
and they get a glimpse of that vulnerable girl who tried so hard for so long
to become anything but
though sometimes the facade slips
and when it does
i run as fast as i can towards people i've never met
so i can try again
that's why there are so many places i can't go back to
too many places have seen the real me
and that's the last thing i need

Rayne Lopez-Gamboa

omniscient observations
being the balance but capable of destruction
like the scale coveted by libra
i still create my paintings like god created man
whose mastery failed within days of first light
while mine live through me
made in my image

being content will still cost you
peace of mind is a myth

Rayne Lopez-Gamboa

limping home like a wounded animal
licking my gashes in private
but does it count
when i still must look everyone in the face and say
that i failed
yet again

Rayne Lopez-Gamboa

i burned a bridge on purpose
i never used it anyway
i danced with my devil
and it gave me the flame
it knows i'm infatuated with fire
i thought you'd know the same
but you asked me why i burned it
why cant i just look the other way
i tell you arson is my pastime
and idle hands are just playthings

Rayne Lopez-Gamboa

the world owes me more than it brings

Rayne Lopez-Gamboa

what terror it is to catch a glimpse of your abuser in the mirror
self loathing because you see them in your reflection
the angle of your cheek in just the right position
can send avalanches down your spine

there are moments
when i break and ask
why didn't i go when i had the chance

what's that feeling? he asked somberly

which one? she answered without looking up from her book

the one where it hurts to watch someone else get everything you ever wanted?

oh, she replied, *life*

steadily i lay the leaves in front of me
as i sit at the edge of the bay
wondering if the sun will set at 6
and if my death will be in vain
there's a ripple in the water
the ghost of it calls my name
the remnants of simple memories
i push back down with a swallow of pain

Rayne Lopez-Gamboa

my mind has tried to shield itself
from things it does not want to remember
things it couldnt handle
but lately memories are becoming unlocked at random
opening pandora's box
once unleashed there's no shoving it back inside
it sits with me on the ledge looking out over the city
holding my hands with tears in my eyes
and it waits for me to recall the little details
the light fixture and the implications
but still i cant fill in all the blanks
it's like a piece of me was stolen
and anyone could be the thief

Rayne Lopez-Gamboa

i gave away my art like it was nothing
just something to remember me by
in some cruel twist of fate im still living
forced to savor all moments
no matter how small
the reminder in my ear always ringing
you almost missed this
you almost missed this

Rayne Lopez-Gamboa

out of the corner of my eyes i see the shadows
the angular hands reaching for my throat
a quick glance in their direction and im jarred back
into a reality where there are no ghosts
but they can hear my thoughts im sure of it
a device recording my every move
my best friend has betrayed me
maybe they all hate me
and my lover has poisoned my food
these thoughts are maggots eating away at me
burrowing through my brain into the other side
my doors are locked my windows are shut
but an intruder could still be inside

Rayne Lopez-Gamboa

i'm fully aware of the talk around town
that i'm a witch and must be burned
judgment without logic is the true crime
if i had the power to challenge god
what the fuck am i doing here

Rayne Lopez-Gamboa

as i look back i realize
it's scary to be a child
everything decided for you
limited knowledge of the world
naive of true danger
i wish i was given more options
given more knowledge
given warnings
i did not receive

Rayne Lopez-Gamboa

1. my fingers tremble at noon as i put them up to my face and although the second hand is red my heart still ticks faster. Anxious.
  2. i'm pale in the morning like a ghost who never found its way back among the tombstones and my eyes are fogged with mist from the dreams of the night before. Tired.
  3. my lungs grew a garden but gave me tainted fruit filled with poisonous nectar and self indulgence. Selfish.
  4. my mind is a tangle of galaxies and stardust, passionate hurricanes and unexpected avalanches never aware of the next strike of lightning. Imaginative.
  5. call me beautiful and you'll be met with the upturned corners of my quivering lips and the shake of a head that doesnt find you sincere. Humble.
  6. my cognizance will find hidden treasures on the infinite white of a canvas unburying small jewels with frayed bristles and a full heart. Passionate.
  7. my hands can hold an eternity of things yet still can't grasp the limit of my body. Dreamer.
  8. my teeth will chatter and my chest will sting yet i still won't let the demons invade my fragile ribcage. Ambitious.
  9. there's nothing more in my veins than belligerent hope and an unrequited love for the vastness of possibilities. Eager.
10. i started as the size of an eye of a needle but so did all fantastical things and what's more belittling than knowing you're just a speck amidst the eye of the universe? Human.

Rayne Lopez-Gamboa

i was up in the tree past 6
picking pears from its limbs
sitting and looking over the pasture
far over the lake during sunset
i have this tingling feeling in my chest
not quite warmth but not quite sadness
i lean over the branch just a bit
straining my eyes to see the horizon
just maybe you were on your way back
bobbing in the water on a sailboat
the golden hour comes and goes
leaving me hungry for closure
i bite a pear, sickly sweet
a basket for you
piled high at my feet

Rayne Lopez-Gamboa

Closing

Argument

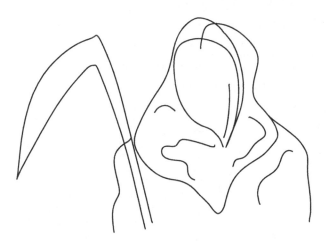

"i was never meant to make it this far anyway"

no one encouraged me
so i steeped in isolation
my ideas submerged longer than recommended
because of this
i had brewed over strength
robust and bold
bitter and spiteful
when i succeed it will taste
rich with notes of florals
i've often wondered that
if no one would have forgotten me
would i have been too weak
to make it

organic growth
looks like vines from ivy
twists and curls plenty
upwards and downwards
juniper and hunter green
if your roots are strong
it won't matter
if it doesn't rain for days

the secret of longevity
is in the rings of a redwood
ripples that tell which years were hardest
some that were rotted out
and yet somehow withstood the pressure
to not cave in completely
knowing it had more purpose
part of a collective system of roots
underneath the surface

Rayne Lopez-Gamboa

there was a time when I believed
the world had magic and it was good

i miss how blissful it felt

Rayne Lopez-Gamboa

i often wonder if death is an illusion
a veil over collective consciousness
ripples in the water when you touch the surface
these hands are not my own
but belong to someone i've never met
i am made up of the succession of simple triumphs
a tangle of fate or a destined chance
my ancestors recognize their face in my features
a pain i haven't yet had to undergo
i'm a walking compilation of moments and places
small pieces of all the lives i will never know

in the end it's my fault, truly it is
i created a scenario neither of us would ever win
you called us star crossed and we knew that was it
bending towards the fall but never grasping at it

Rayne Lopez-Gamboa

wrath comes in waves
it sucks me down to drown

Rayne Lopez-Gamboa

save yourself the torment
if you had to do it again

don't choose me

Rayne Lopez-Gamboa

my last breath will be a sigh of relief

the storm must calm
or risk becoming too powerful
to regain control

Rayne Lopez-Gamboa

i've waited too long to change
let myself make mistakes haphazardly
resisting any safe haven or hand to hold
i was wrong and i regret it
but is it really my fault for trying to make
my life my own

Rayne Lopez-Gamboa

what im guilty of is self indulgence
hedonism is my religion
too often i've been restricted by
outcomes
circumstances
expectations
all morals are objective
if i bend their will to my own

Rayne Lopez-Gamboa

i've been sentenced to purgatory
sitting idle while others move ahead
like game pieces they pass me
waiting to catch up
except i keep pulling cards that skip my turn
or send me back to start

Rayne Lopez-Gamboa

i refuse to continue the cycle
that expects shame to keep you quiet
and obedience to get my approval
you will run as far as you like
through fields of marigolds and daisies
there will still be storms to endure
but if you decide it's not for you
i'll be waiting here just the same

Rayne Lopez-Gamboa

it's not the will to live that's saved me
it's a fear that they'll forget me

Rayne Lopez-Gamboa

i missed out on a lot of love
simply because
i locked myself inside my mental prison
convincing myself i was unworthy
sentencing myself to isolation
when the punishment didn't fit the crime

Rayne Lopez-Gamboa

don't forget that this is reality
the shadow from the smoke alarm looks like a half
moon on your white wall
just above framed picture of the two of you
distorted faces in the dark
quickly ground yourself to make sure you're really in
your body
looking for a reminder that you're chained to it even if
you don't feel the pull
to convince your soul that this is where you belong
even though you were born from stardust
and pieces of your soul were fragmented
from endless reincarnation

Rayne Lopez-Gamboa

there are intrusive thoughts i dare tell no one
things that make me question my sanity
for my safety i cannot utter them
the mere mention will manifest reality

Rayne Lopez-Gamboa

i find it hard to admit my wrongdoings
but if i cant see them then they're not there
i live in the space between good and evil
and i have been for years
it must have a name but it escapes me
for the horizon where heaven meets hell
in the fuzzy line where morals blur into faults
i am existing with a hedonist's will

i have a distorted sense of self
that's not my face in the mirror
my hands have done things that they've kept secret from each other
i pour over the possibilities in my head
why i am the way i am
overwhelmed with the responses to my own question
i delicately place my head in my hands
then firmly squeeze on either side
to try and kill the images of a dismal fate
that i have cultivated
by keeping my demons warm and fed

Rayne Lopez-Gamboa

self-awareness is key
to balance or misery
and stability was never my strong suit

Made in the USA
Middletown, DE
13 July 2024

57219033R10064